contents

NZ, Canada, US and UK readers
Please note that Australian cup and
spoon measurements are metric.
A conversion chart appears on page 62.

ciabatta with olive and herb paste

1 loaf ciabatta bread (440g)
2 tablespoons olive oil
olive and herb paste
250g seeded green olives
½ small white onion (40g), chopped coarsely
freshly ground black pepper
1 clove garlic, crushed
¼ cup (60ml) extra virgin olive oil
1 tablespoon coarsely chopped fresh flat-leaf parsley
1 teaspoon coarsely chopped fresh oregano
1 teaspoon lime juice

1 Preheat oven to 200°C/180°C fan-forced.
2 Meanwhile, make olive and herb paste.
3 Cut bread into 1cm slices. Place bread, in single layer, on oven trays; brush with oil. Bake about 5 minutes each side or until browned lightly and crisp; cool.
4 Serve ciabatta with olive and herb paste.
olive and herb paste Process olives, onion, pepper and garlic into a coarse paste; gradually add oil, in a thin steady stream, while motor is operating. Stir in herbs and juice.

preparation time 20 minutes
cooking time 10 minutes
serves 6
per serving 19.4g fat; 1845kJ (441 cal)
tip Olive and herb paste can be prepared a day ahead and refrigerated.

beetroot tzatziki   sweet chilli dip

beetroot tzatziki

2 large beetroot (400g)
1 cup (280g) yogurt
½ cup (100g) ricotta cheese
2 cloves garlic, crushed
2 tablespoons lemon juice
¼ cup finely chopped
   fresh chives
¼ cup finely chopped
   fresh mint

1 Place unpeeled beetroot in disposable baking dish. Cook in covered barbecue, using indirect heat, following manufacturer's instructions, about 1 hour or until tender; cool.
2 Peel beetroot; chop coarsely. Place beetroot in food processor with yogurt, cheese, garlic and juice; blend until combined.
3 Remove from processor; stir in herbs.

preparation time 15 minutes
(plus cooling time)
cooking time 1 hour
serves 6
per serving 3.6g fat; 362kJ (87 cal)
tip Wear a pair of rubber gloves when you handle the cooked beetroot to avoid staining your hands.

sweet chilli dip

250g softened cream cheese
¼ cup (60ml) sweet chilli sauce
1 tablespoon finely chopped
   fresh coriander

1 Combine ingredients in small bowl.
2 Serve with grissini (breadsticks), crackers or vegetable sticks, if desired.

preparation time 5 minutes
serves 4
per serving 21.1g fat; 954kJ (228 cal)

spicy tomato salsa

4 medium tomatoes (760g),
  chopped finely
2 cloves garlic, crushed
1 small brown onion (80g),
  sliced thinly
1 teaspoon cajun seasoning
2 teaspoons no-added-salt
  tomato paste

1 Combine ingredients in small saucepan.
2 Cook, stirring, over medium heat about
15 minutes or until onion is soft and sauce
has thickened; cool.

preparation time 10 minutes
cooking time 15 minutes
serves 4
per serving 0.4g fat; 153kJ (37 cal)

baba ghanoush

2 small eggplants (460g)
⅓ cup (95g) low-fat yogurt
1 tablespoon lemon juice
2 cloves garlic, crushed
1 teaspoon tahini
1 teaspoon ground cumin
½ teaspoon sesame oil
2 tablespoons finely chopped
  fresh coriander

1 Preheat oven to 200°C/180°C fan-forced.
2 Halve eggplants lengthways; place on oven
tray. Bake about 35 minutes or until tender.
3 Cool; remove and discard skin. Blend or
process eggplant with remaining ingredients
until smooth. Cover; refrigerate 30 minutes.

preparation time 10 minutes
(plus refrigeration time)
cooking time 35 minutes
serves 4
per serving 2.2g fat; 218kJ (52 cal)

quick beetroot dip

225g can sliced beetroot,
  drained well
¼ cup (70g) low-fat yogurt
1 teaspoon ground coriander
2 teaspoons ground cumin

1 Blend or process ingredients until combined.

preparation time 10 minutes
serves 4
per serving 0.6g fat; 137kJ (33 cal)

from top spicy tomato salsa,
baba ghanoush, quick beetroot dip

tomato salsa   eggplant parsley dip

tomato salsa

3 medium tomatoes (570g),
seeded, chopped finely
1 small avocado (200g),
chopped finely
1 medium red onion (170g),
chopped finely
2 fresh small red thai chillies,
chopped finely
2 tablespoons coarsely
chopped fresh coriander
130g can corn kernels,
rinsed, drained
1 tablespoon lemon juice

1 Combine ingredients in medium bowl.
2 Serve with corn chips or baked flour tortilla wedges, if desired.

preparation time 15 minutes
serves 6
per serving 5.5g fat; 375kJ (90 cal)

eggplant parsley dip

1 large eggplant (500g)
1 medium white onion (150g),
chopped finely
2 tablespoons yogurt
2 cloves garlic, crushed
1 tablespoon red wine vinegar
2 tablespoons olive oil
½ cup finely chopped fresh
flat-leaf parsley

1 Prick eggplant all over with fork; place in disposable baking dish. Cook in covered barbecue, using indirect heat, following manufacturer's instructions, about 1 hour or until soft. When cool enough to handle, halve eggplant; scoop out flesh. Chop flesh coarsely; discard skin.
2 Blend or process eggplant, onion, yogurt, garlic, vinegar and oil until chopped coarsely.
3 Add parsley; blend until just combined. Refrigerate until cold.

preparation time 15 minutes
(plus refrigeration time)
cooking time 1 hour
serves 6
per serving 6.6g fat; 348kJ (83 cal)

9

red onion and balsamic jam

¼ cup (60ml) olive oil
3 medium red onions (510g),
 sliced thinly
¼ cup (50g) firmly packed
 brown sugar
⅓ cup (80ml) balsamic vinegar
½ teaspoon dill seeds
¼ cup (60ml) chicken stock

1 Heat oil in medium saucepan; cook onion, stirring, until soft and browned lightly.
2 Stir in sugar, vinegar, seeds and stock. Simmer, uncovered, about 20 minutes or until mixture thickens.

preparation time 10 minutes
cooking time 20 minutes
makes 1½ cups
per tablespoon 3.1g fat; 198kJ (47 cal)
tip This jam is suitable to serve with lamb and chicken.

garlic and hoisin sauce

1 whole bulb garlic
½ cup (125ml) hoisin sauce
2 tablespoons sweet chilli sauce
1 tablespoon soy sauce
1 tablespoon rice vinegar
1 teaspoon sesame oil
2 tablespoons coarsely
 chopped fresh coriander

1 Place garlic in disposable baking tray; cook in covered barbecue, using indirect heat, following manufacturer's instructions, about 45 minutes or until cloves are tender. When cool enough to handle, squeeze out garlic.
2 Combine garlic in medium bowl with sauces, vinegar and oil; whisk until smooth. Stir in coriander.

preparation time 10 minutes
cooking time 45 minutes
makes 1 cup
per tablespoon 1.2g fat; 147kJ (35 cal)
tip This Asian-style sauce goes well with pork, beef, lamb or chicken, and is good brushed over kebabs.

red onion and balsamic jam   garlic and hoisin sauce

chilli and coriander sauce

creamy avocado dip

chilli and coriander sauce

2 large tomatoes (500g),
   chopped coarsely
¼ cup (60ml) water
⅓ cup (80ml) lime juice
¼ cup (55g) firmly packed
   brown sugar
1 teaspoon fish sauce
⅓ cup (80ml) sweet chilli sauce
2 tablespoons coarsely
   chopped fresh coriander

1 Combine tomato, the water, juice, sugar and sauces in medium pan; stir over low heat until sugar dissolves. Bring to a boil; reduce heat. Simmer, uncovered, about 10 minutes or until sauce thickens.
2 Remove from heat; cool. Stir in coriander.

preparation time 5 minutes
cooking time 15 minutes
makes 1 cup
per tablespoon 0.3g fat; 127kJ (30 cal)

creamy avocado dip

1 large avocado (320g)
¼ cup (60g) sour cream
¼ cup (75g) mayonnaise
2 tablespoons olive oil
1 teaspoon Tabasco sauce
1 clove garlic, quartered
¼ cup tightly packed fresh
   coriander leaves
1 tablespoon lemon juice

1 Blend or process ingredients until smooth.

preparation time 5 minutes
makes 1½ cups
per tablespoon 7.5g fat; 303kJ (72 cal)

black olive paste

4 cloves coarsely chopped garlic
4 cups seeded black olives
5 drained anchovy fillets
1 tablespoon rinsed, drained capers
½ cup coarsely chopped fresh flat-leaf parsley
1 tablespoon coarsely chopped fresh oregano
1 cup extra virgin olive oil

1 Blend or process garlic, olives, anchovy, capers and herbs until chopped finely. Gradually add oil, in a thin steady stream, while motor is operating; process until smooth.
2 Spoon into hot sterilised jar. Cover with a thin layer of extra oil; seal.

preparation time 15 minutes
makes 3½ cups
per tablespoon 8.3g fat; 355kJ (85 cal)
tip Paste can be refrigerated for up to three weeks.

pesto bread

1 loaf ciabatta bread (440g)
¼ cup (60ml) olive oil
¼ cup (65g) basil pesto
¼ cup (65g) char-grilled vegetable pesto

1 Cut bread diagonally into 12 slices. Brush bread slices lightly with oil.
2 Cook bread on heated oiled barbecue (or grill or grill plate), uncovered, until toasted lightly both sides.
3 Spread half the bread slices with basil pesto; spread remaining slices with char-grilled vegetable pesto.

preparation time 10 minutes
cooking time 5 minutes
serves 6
per serving 19.3g fat; 1577kJ (377 cal)
tip We used bottled basil pesto and char-grilled vegetable pesto, available from most supermarkets.

bruschetta

2 large tomatoes (500g), chopped coarsely
1 small red onion (100g), chopped finely
1 clove garlic, crushed
2 tablespoons olive oil
½ teaspoon white sugar
2 tablespoons finely shredded fresh basil
1 loaf ciabatta bread (440g)
¼ cup (60ml) olive oil, extra

1 Combine tomato, onion, garlic, oil, sugar and basil in medium bowl.
2 Cut bread into 1.5cm thick slices; brush with extra oil. Cook bread on heated oiled barbecue (or grill or grill plate), uncovered, until toasted lightly both sides.
3 Serve tomato mixture on toasted bread.

preparation time 15 minutes
cooking time 5 minutes
serves 6
per serving 17.7g fat; 1554kJ (371 cal)

oven-baked vegetable crisps

cooking-oil spray
4 medium parsnips (1kg)
4 medium potatoes (800g)
1 medium kumara (400g)
2 teaspoons sea salt

1 Preheat oven to 160°C/140°C fan-forced. Spray three oven trays with cooking-oil spray.
2 Using mandolin, v-slicer or sharp knife, cut parsnip, potato and kumara into 2mm slices.
3 Place parsnip, in single layer, on oven trays; lightly coat with cooking-oil spray. Bake, uncovered, about 40 minutes or until browned both sides and crisp. Turn onto wire rack to cool.
4 Repeat step three using potato then kumara.
5 Sprinkle crisps with salt.

preparation time 15 minutes
cooking time 2 hours
serves 8
per serving 1.3g fat; 555kJ (133 cal)
tips The thinner the slices, the faster they'll become crisp, so some crisps may need to be removed from the oven before others. If you don't have a fan-forced oven, rotate oven trays frequently to ensure the vegetable slices brown evenly.

crisp garlic wedges and pesto dip

1 cup firmly packed, coarsely chopped fresh basil
1 clove garlic, crushed
2 tablespoons roasted pine nuts
2 tablespoons finely grated fresh parmesan cheese
2 tablespoons olive oil
2 teaspoons lemon juice
1¼ cups (300g) sour cream
crisp garlic wedges
4 large pitta breads
150g butter, melted
2 cloves garlic, crushed
⅔ cup (50g) finely grated fresh parmesan cheese

1 Preheat oven to 200°C/180°C fan-forced.
2 Make crisp garlic wedges.
3 Blend or process basil, garlic, nuts, cheese, oil and juice until smooth. Combine in medium bowl with sour cream.
4 Serve with crisp garlic wedges.
crisp garlic wedges Split pitta in half; cut into large wedges. Place pitta, split-side up, on oven trays. Brush with combined butter and garlic; sprinkle with cheese. Bake about 8 minutes or until browned lightly and crisp.

preparation time 10 minutes
cooking time 25 minutes
serves 6
per serving 54.5g fat; 2696kJ (644 cal)
tip Crisp garlic wedges can be made a week ahead and stored in an airtight container or frozen for up to two months.

polenta

2 litres (8 cups) water
2 teaspoons salt
2 cups (340g) polenta
¼ cup (60ml) olive oil

1 Combine the water and salt in large saucepan; bring to a boil. Gradually sprinkle polenta over water, stirring constantly with wooden spoon until smooth.
2 Reduce heat to low; cook, stirring, about 30 minutes or until polenta is very thick and spoon can stand upright in centre.
3 Spoon mixture evenly into greased 20cm x 30cm lamington pan; stand at room temperature 3 hours or until cold.
4 Turn polenta out of pan; cut into 4cm slices. Heat oil in large frying pan until very hot; reduce heat. Gently fry polenta slices until golden brown both sides.

preparation time 15 minutes (plus standing time)
cooking time 50 minutes
serves 4
per serving 15.4g fat; 1678kJ (401 cal)
tip This is a specialty of northern Italy and is particularly popular around Venice. Served plain, it is often accompanied by bolognese sauce. Hot, fried polenta can also be topped with anchovies and sliced olives or other toppings.

parmesan crisps

1 cup finely grated parmesan cheese
¼ teaspoon finely ground black pepper
1 teaspoon dried oregano

1 Preheat oven to 200°C/180°C fan-forced.
2 Combine ingredients in medium bowl. Place 2 teaspoons of mixture, 3cm apart, on baking-paper-lined oven trays; flatten with fingertips. Bake, uncovered, 4 minutes; cool on trays.

preparation time 5 minutes
cooking time 25 minutes
makes 18
per serving 1.4g fat; 82kJ (19 cal)
tips Crisps can be made three days ahead and stored in an airtight container. These crisps can also be made in two large sheets; break into shards to serve.
The flavourings can be omitted and the plain cheese crisps topped with olive paste and a little sour cream for finger food.

moroccan-style lamb cutlets

24 french-trimmed lamb cutlets
¼ cup (40g) moroccan seasoning
250g prepared baba ghanoush
2 teaspoons cumin seeds, toasted

1 Lightly coat lamb with seasoning. Cook lamb on heated oiled barbecue (or grill or grill plate), uncovered, until browned both sides and cooked as desired.
2 Top each lamb cutlet with a teaspoon of baba ghanoush and a few cumin seeds.

preparation time 10 minutes
cooking time 10 minutes
makes 24
per cutlet 5.7g fat; 394kJ (94 cal)
tips Moroccan seasoning, a spice mixture including turmeric, cinnamon and cumin, adds an authentic Moroccan flavouring to dishes. It is available at supermarkets.
Baba ghanoush is a Middle Eastern-style eggplant dip, also available at supermarkets or delicatessens.
To garnish cutlets, dip trimmed green onion stems briefly into boiling water; tie around cutlet bones.

lamb kofta with chilli and yogurt sauce

1kg lean lamb mince
1 large brown onion (200g),
    chopped finely
1 clove garlic, crushed
1 tablespoon ground cumin
2 teaspoons ground turmeric
2 teaspoons ground allspice
1 tablespoon finely chopped
    fresh mint
2 tablespoons finely chopped
    fresh flat-leaf parsley
1 egg, beaten lightly
6 pocket pitta bread,
    quartered
yogurt sauce
¾ cup (200g) low-fat yogurt
1 clove garlic, crushed
1 tablespoon finely chopped
    fresh flat-leaf parsley
chilli tomato sauce
¼ cup (60ml) tomato sauce
¼ cup (60ml) chilli sauce

1 Combine lamb, onion, garlic, spices, herbs and egg in large bowl; shape mixture into 18 balls. Mould balls around skewers to form sausage shapes.

2 Cook kofta, in batches, on heated oiled grill plate (or grill or barbecue) until browned all over and cooked through.

3 Meanwhile, make yogurt sauce; make chilli tomato sauce.

4 Serve kofta with pitta, yogurt sauce and chilli tomato sauce. Serve with tabbouleh, if desired.

yogurt sauce Combine ingredients in small bowl.

chilli tomato sauce Combine sauces in small bowl.

preparation time 20 minutes
cooking time 10 minutes
serves 6
per serving 14.5g fat; 1817kJ (435 cal)
tips You need to soak 18 bamboo skewers in water for at least an hour before use, to prevent them from splintering and scorching during cooking.

tandoori lamb cutlets

½ cup (150g) tandoori paste
¾ cup (200g) yogurt
12 lamb cutlets (900g)
chutney
1 tablespoon vegetable oil
1 small red onion (100g), chopped finely
2 large tomatoes (500g), chopped finely
1 tablespoon lime juice
1 tablespoon sweet chilli sauce
2 tablespoons finely chopped fresh coriander
raita
1 lebanese cucumber (130g), seeded, chopped finely
2 tablespoons finely chopped fresh mint
¾ cup (200g) yogurt

1 Combine paste and yogurt in large bowl, add lamb; toss to cover completely in mixture.
2 Cook lamb on heated oiled grill plate (or grill or barbecue), in batches, until browned both sides and cooked as desired.
3 Meanwhile, make chutney; make raita.
4 Serve lamb with separate bowls of chutney and raita. Top with thinly sliced green onion, if desired.
chutney Combine ingredients in small bowl.
raita Combine ingredients in small bowl.

preparation time 20 minutes
cooking time 10 minutes
serves 4
per serving 49.4g fat; 2553kJ (611 cal)
tip Lamb can be marinated a day ahead and refrigerated, covered.

pork spring rolls with chilli plum sauce

6 dried shiitake mushrooms

200g pork mince

2 wombok leaves,
    shredded finely

1 trimmed celery stalk (100g),
    shredded finely

1 small carrot (70g),
    grated finely

½ cup (40g) bean sprouts

1 green onion, sliced thinly

1 tablespoon finely chopped
    fresh coriander

1 teaspoon peanut oil

1 clove garlic, crushed

1 tablespoon light soy sauce

1 tablespoon oyster sauce

36 x 12.5mm square spring
    roll wrappers

1 egg, beaten lightly

vegetable oil for deep-frying

chilli plum sauce

1 cup (250ml) plum sauce

1 tablespoon soy sauce

3cm piece fresh ginger (15g),
    grated

1 fresh small red thai chilli,
    chopped finely

1 Place mushrooms in heatproof bowl, cover with boiling water; stand 20 minutes, drain. Discard stems from mushrooms, chop caps finely.

2 Combine mushrooms with remaining ingredients, except wrappers, egg and vegetable oil, in large bowl; mix well.

3 For each roll, place 2 teaspoons of filling across one corner of wrapper. Brush edges of wrapper with a little egg, tuck in ends and roll up to enclose filling.

4 Heat vegetable oil in large saucepan until hot; deep-fry spring rolls, in batches, until golden brown and cooked through. Drain on absorbent paper.

5 Meanwhile, make chilli plum sauce.

6 Serve spring rolls with chilli plum sauce.

chilli plum sauce Combine ingredients in small bowl.

preparation time 30 minutes
(plus standing time)
cooking time 20 minutes
makes 36
per spring roll 2.4g fat; 265kJ (63 cal)
tips The filling can be made several hours ahead. Rolls can be made up to two hours ahead. Place in a single layer on tray lined with plastic wrap; cover and refrigerate. Deep-fry just before serving.

tandoori drumsticks

12 chicken drumsticks (1.8kg)
½ cup (140g) yogurt
2 teaspoons ground cumin
2 teaspoons ground coriander
1 teaspoon sweet paprika
2 cloves garlic, crushed
few drops red food colouring
½ cup (160g) lime pickle
½ cup (160g) mango chutney

1   Score each chicken drumstick three times.
2   Combine yogurt, spices, garlic and food colouring in large bowl;
add chicken. Cover; refrigerate 3 hours or overnight.
3   Cook undrained chicken on heated oiled barbecue (or grill or grill
plate), uncovered, until browned all over and cooked through.
4   Serve chicken with pickle and chutney.

preparation time 10 minutes (plus refrigeration time)
cooking time 20 minutes
serves 4
per serving 40.7g fat; 2855kJ (682 cal)
tip Lime pickle is an Indian condiment of limes that adds a hot and spicy
taste to meals. It is available from most Asian and Indian food stores.

vietnamese spring rolls

1 medium red capsicum (200g)
1 medium carrot (120g)
1 tablespoon peanut oil
700g chicken breast fillets
4cm piece fresh ginger (20g), grated
2 cloves garlic, crushed
4 green onions, chopped finely
100g bean thread noodles
1 tablespoon finely chopped vietnamese mint
500g buk choy, shredded finely
¼ cup (60ml) sweet chilli sauce
1 tablespoon soy sauce
40 spring roll wrappers
peanut oil, for deep-frying
chilli lime dipping sauce
⅓ cup (80ml) sweet chilli sauce
2 tablespoons lime juice
3 green onions, chopped finely

1 Halve capsicum; discard seeds and membrane. Slice capsicum and carrot into paper-thin strips.

2 Heat half the oil in medium saucepan; cook chicken, in batches, until browned and cooked through. Cool 10 minutes; shred finely.

3 Heat remaining oil in same pan; cook ginger, garlic and onion, stirring, about 2 minutes or until onion is soft.

4 Meanwhile, place noodles in large heatproof bowl, cover with boiling water; stand 2 minutes, drain. Chop noodles coarsely.

5 Combine capsicum, carrot, chicken, onion mixture and noodles in large bowl with mint, buk choy and sauces.

6 Place a rounded tablespoon of the mixture across edge of one wrapper; fold in ends then roll to enclose filling. Place on tray, seam-side down. Repeat with remaining mixture and wrappers, placing on tray in single layer.

7 Make chilli lime dipping sauce.

8 Just before serving, heat oil in wok; deep-fry spring rolls, in batches, until golden brown and cooked through. Drain on absorbent paper; serve with dipping sauce.

chilli lime dipping sauce Combine ingredients in small bowl.

preparation time 1 hour
cooking time 25 minutes
makes 40
per roll 4.3g fat; 307kJ (73 cal)

basil prawns with avocado mash

1kg large uncooked prawns
½ cup coarsely chopped
   fresh basil
2 cloves garlic, crushed
1 tablespoon finely
   grated lime rind
avocado mash
2 medium avocados (500g)
2 tablespoons lime juice
2 medium tomatoes (380g),
   seeded, chopped finely
1 small red onion (100g),
   chopped finely
2 teaspoons ground cumin
2 tablespoons finely chopped
   fresh basil
2 fresh small red thai chillies,
   chopped finely

1 Shell and devein prawns, leaving tails
intact. Combine prawns, basil, garlic and
rind in large bowl. Cover; refrigerate 3 hours
or overnight.

2 Cook prawns on heated oiled barbecue
(or grill or grill plate), uncovered, until changed
in colour and just cooked through.

3 Meanwhile, make avocado mash.

4 Serve prawns with avocado mash and
lime wedges, if desired.

avocado mash Mash flesh of one avocado
in small bowl until almost smooth. Coarsely
chop flesh of remaining avocado; add to
bowl of mashed avocado with remaining
ingredients; mix well.

preparation time 30 minutes
(plus refrigerating time)
cooking time 10 minutes
serves 4
per serving 20.8g fat; 1320kJ (315 cal)

fresh rice paper rolls with prawns

500g cooked medium prawns
1 cup (80g) finely shredded
  wombok
½ cup (120g) coarsely
  grated carrot
2 tablespoons coarsely
  chopped fresh mint
2 tablespoons coarsely
  chopped fresh coriander
12 x 16cm-round
  rice paper wrappers
dipping sauce
⅓ cup (75g) caster sugar
¼ cup (60ml) white vinegar
¼ cup (60ml) water
2 teaspoons fish sauce
2 fresh small red thai chillies,
  sliced thinly
1 tablespoon coarsely
  chopped fresh coriander

1 Shell and devein prawns. Combine wombok,
carrot, mint and coriander in large bowl.
2 Cover a board with a damp tea towel. Place
one sheet of rice paper in medium bowl of
warm water until softened; place on tea towel.
Place a tablespoon of the mixture in centre of
rice paper; top with two prawns. Fold in ends,
then roll wrapper to enclose filling. Repeat with
remaining ingredients. Cover rolls with a damp
paper towel to prevent them from drying out.
3 Make dipping sauce.
4 Serve rolls with dipping sauce.
dipping sauce Place sugar, vinegar and
the water in small saucepan; stir over medium
heat until sugar dissolves. Bring to a boil;
remove from heat. Stir in sauce and chilli;
cool. Stir in coriander.

preparation time 30 minutes
cooking time 5 minutes
makes 12
per roll 0.3g fat; 220kJ (53 cal)
tip The rolls can be made up to four hours
ahead. Keep fresh by covering with damp
absorbent paper towel.

saffron prawns

1kg uncooked king prawns
1½ cups (225g) plain flour
½ teaspoon salt
1½ cups (375ml) light beer
pinch saffron threads
vegetable oil, for deep-frying
lemon wedges, for serving

1 Peel and devein prawns, leaving tails intact.
2 Sift flour and salt into large bowl; whisk in beer and saffron until smooth.
3 Pat prawns dry with absorbent paper. Dip prawns in batter, in batches; drain excess batter. Heat oil in large saucepan until hot; deep-fry prawns until changed in colour and just cooked through. Remove prawns; drain thoroughly on absorbent paper.
4 Repeat with remaining prawns and batter. Serve immediately with lemon wedges.

preparation time 15 minutes
cooking time 10 minutes
serves 8
per serving 5.5g fat; 873kJ (208 cal)
tip Recipe is best made just before serving.

deep-fried whitebait

1 cup (150g) plain flour
¼ cup coarsely chopped
   fresh basil
1 teaspoon garlic salt
500g whitebait
vegetable oil, for deep-frying
spiced mayonnaise dip
1 cup (300g) mayonnaise
2 cloves garlic, crushed
2 tablespoons lemon juice
1 tablespoon rinsed, drained
   capers, chopped finely
1 tablespoon coarsely
   chopped fresh
      flat-leaf parsley

1   Combine flour, basil and garlic salt in large bowl. Toss whitebait in flour mixture, in batches, until coated.
2   Heat oil in medium saucepan; deep-fry whitebait, in batches, until browned and cooked through, drain on absorbent paper.
3   Meanwhile, make spiced mayonnaise dip.
4   Serve whitebait with spiced mayonnaise dip.
spiced mayonnaise dip Combine ingredients in small serving bowl.

preparation time 10 minutes
cooking time 15 minutes
serves 4
per serving 48.1g fat; 2966kJ (709 cal)

potatoes with aïoli

1kg kipfler potatoes
aïoli
2 egg yolks
2 tablespoons lemon juice
2 cloves garlic, crushed
¾ cup (180ml) olive oil
1 tablespoon hot water

1 Make aïoli.
2 Cut potatoes in half lengthways.
3 Cook potato on heated oiled barbecue (or grill or grill plate)
until tender; serve with aïoli.
aïoli Blend or process egg yolks, juice and garlic until combined.
With motor operating, gradually add oil, in a thin steady stream;
process until thick. Stir in the water.

preparation time 20 minutes
cooking time 20 minutes
serves 4
per serving 44.1g fat; 2346kJ (561 cal)
tip Aïoli can be made a day ahead and refrigerated, covered.

vegetable rice paper rolls

50g vermicelli noodles
2 medium avocados (500g)
1 medium carrot (120g)
100g garlic chives
24 small round rice paper
    wrappers
3 red radishes (100g),
    grated coarsely
1 cup (80g) bean sprouts,
    trimmed
24 large mint leaves
chilli dipping sauce
½ cup (125ml) white vinegar
1 cup (220g) caster sugar
1 teaspoon salt
¼ cup (60ml) water
1 clove garlic, crushed
½ small red onion (50g),
    chopped finely
½ lebanese cucumber (60g),
    seeded, chopped finely
1 tablespoon finely chopped
    fresh coriander
1 fresh small red thai chilli,
    chopped finely
1 tablespoon cashews,
    roasted, chopped coarsely

1 Place noodles in medium bowl of hot water for 10 minutes or until softened; drain well.
2 Meanwhile, make chilli dipping sauce.
3 Thinly slice avocado. Cut carrot into long thin strips. Cut garlic chives into the same lengths as carrot.
4 Cover a board with a damp tea towel. Place one sheet of rice paper in a bowl of warm water until softened; place on tea towel. Place a slice of avocado, some of the carrot, radish, sprouts, a mint leaf, some garlic chives and noodles in the centre of the sheet.
5 Fold bottom half of the rice paper up. Fold in one side; roll over to enclose filling. Repeat with remaining sheets and ingredients. Place rolls on oven tray lined with plastic wrap; cover with damp absorbent paper towel and refrigerate until ready to serve.
6 Serve with chilli dipping sauce.
chilli dipping sauce Bring vinegar, sugar, salt and the water to a boil in small saucepan; boil, uncovered, 2 minutes. Pour vinegar mixture over remaining ingredients in medium bowl. Cool to room temperature.

preparation time 40 minutes
cooking time 2 minutes
makes 24
per roll 3.7g fat; 388kJ (93 cal)
tips The dipping sauce can be made a day ahead; keep covered in the refrigerator. The rolls can be made up to four hours ahead. Keep fresh by covering with damp absorbent paper towel.

coconut and vanilla parfait

⅓ cup (80ml) coconut cream
1.5 litres vanilla ice-cream,
    softened
2 tablespoons
    passionfruit pulp
⅓ cup (15g) flaked
    coconut, toasted

1 Combine coconut cream and ice-cream in large bowl.
2 Divide mixture evenly between four parfait glasses. Top each parfait with passionfruit pulp and coconut.

preparation time 10 minutes
serves 4
per serving 22.9g fat; 1574kJ (376 cal)

marsala and almond mascarpone

250g mascarpone
2 tablespoons marsala
⅓ cup (55g) sugared almonds, chopped coarsely
½ cup (125ml) thickened cream, whipped
1 tablespoon honey
4 sponge finger biscuits

1   Combine mascarpone, marsala, nuts, cream and honey in medium bowl.
2   Spoon mascarpone mixture into individual serving glasses. Serve with biscuits.

preparation time 10 minutes
serves 4
per serving 52.9g fat; 2515kJ (601 cal)

pistachio bread

3 egg whites
⅓ cup (75g) white sugar
¼ teaspoon ground cardamom
1 teaspoon finely grated orange rind
¾ cup (110g) plain flour
¾ cup (110g) pistachios

1 Preheat oven to 180°C/160°C fan-forced. Grease 8cm x 26cm bar pan; line base and sides with baking paper, extending paper 5cm above long sides of pan.
2 Beat egg whites in small bowl with electric mixer until soft peaks form. With motor operating, gradually add sugar, beating until dissolved between additions. Fold in cardamom, rind, flour and nuts; spread mixture into pan.
3 Bake about 30 minutes or until browned lightly; cool in pan. Wrap in foil; stand overnight.
4 Preheat oven to 150°C/130°C fan-forced.
5 Using a serrated or electric knife, cut bread on an angle into 3mm slices. Place slices on ungreased oven trays. Bake about 15 minutes or until dry and crisp; turn onto wire rack to cool.

preparation time 10 minutes (plus standing and cooling time)
cooking time 45 minutes
makes 35 slices
per slice 1.6g fat; 158kJ (38 cal)
tips Uncut bread can be frozen after the first baking. After the second baking, bread slices can be stored up to four days in an airtight container. For a different spiced version, substitute the cardamom with ½ teaspoon ground cinnamon and ¼ teaspoon ground nutmeg.

greek almond biscuits

3 cups (375g) almond meal
1 cup (220g) caster sugar
3 drops almond essence
3 egg whites, beaten lightly
1 cup (80g) flaked almonds

1 Preheat oven to 180°C/160°C fan-forced.
2 Combine almond meal, sugar and essence in large bowl. Add egg whites; stir until mixture forms a firm paste.
3 Roll level tablespoons of mixture into flaked almonds; roll into 8cm logs. Press on any remaining almonds. Shape logs to form crescents; place on baking-paper-lined oven trays. Bake about 15 minutes or until browned lightly; cool on trays.

preparation time 30 minutes (plus cooling time)
cooking time 15 minutes
makes 25
per biscuit 10.1g fat; 595kJ (142 cal)
tip Biscuits can be made a week ahead and are suitable to freeze.

glossary

allspice also known as pimento or jamaican pepper; tastes like a blend of cinnamon, clove and nutmeg – all spices.

almonds flat, pointy-ended nuts with a creamy white kernel that is covered by a brown skin.

meal also known as ground almonds; nuts are powdered to a coarse flour-like texture.

basil an aromatic herb; there are many types, but the most commonly used is sweet basil.

bean sprouts also known as bean shoots; tender new growths of assorted beans and seeds. The most readily available are mung bean, soy bean, alfalfa and snow pea sprouts.

beetroot also known as red beets or just beets; firm, round root vegetable.

buk choy also called pak choi or chinese white cabbage; has a fresh, mild mustard taste and is good braised or in stir-fries. *Baby buk choy* is also available and is slightly more tender than buk choy.

butter use salted or unsalted (sweet) butter; 125g is equal to one stick of butter.

cajun seasoning a blend of assorted herbs and spices that can include paprika, basil, onion, fennel, thyme, cayenne and tarragon.

capers the grey-green buds of a warm climate (usually Mediterranean) shrub; sold either dried and salted or pickled in a vinegar brine. Capers should be rinsed well before using.

capsicum also known as bell pepper or, simply, pepper. Discard membranes and seeds before use.

cheese

cream commonly known as Philadelphia or Philly; a soft cow-milk cheese.

mascarpone a buttery-rich, cream-like cheese made from cows' milk.

parmesan also known as parmigiano; a hard, grainy cow-milk cheese.

ricotta a sweet, moist, soft white cow-milk cheese with a slightly grainy texture.

chilli available in many types and sizes. Use rubber gloves when seeding and chopping fresh chillies as they can burn your skin. Removing seeds and membranes lessens the heat level.

red thai also known as "scuds"; small, hot and bright red in colour.

coconut

cream the first pressing of the coconut flesh, without the addition of water. Available in cans and cartons at supermarkets.

flaked dried, flaked coconut flesh.

coriander also known as pak chee, cilantro or chinese parsley; bright-green leafy herb with a pungent flavour. Both the stems and roots of coriander can also be used. Coriander seeds cannot be substituted for the fresh herb, as the taste is very different.

cucumber, lebanese short, slender and thin-skinned. Probably the most popular variety because of its tender, edible skin, tiny, yielding seeds and sweet, fresh and flavoursome taste.

cumin also known as zeera or comino.

eggplant also known as aubergine.

flour, plain an all-purpose flour made from wheat.

garlic chives also known as chinese chives; have rougher, flatter leaves than simple chives, and possess a pink-tinged teardrop-shaped flowering bud at the end.

ginger also known as green or root ginger; the thick root of a tropical plant.

kumara Polynesian name of orange-fleshed sweet potato.

mince also known as ground meat as in beef, chicken, pork or lamb.

noodles

bean thread made with mung bean flour; very fine, almost transparent noodles. Also known as bean thread vermicelli, or cellophane or glass noodles.

vermicelli also known as sen mee, mei fun or bee hoon; similar to bean threads, only longer and made with rice flour instead of mung bean starch.

paprika ground dried red capsicum (bell pepper); there are many types available, including sweet, hot, mild and smoked.

parsley flat-leaf also known as continental parsley or italian parsley.

pistachio green, delicately flavoured nuts inside hard off-white shells. Available salted or unsalted.

polenta also known as cornmeal; a flour-like cereal made of dried corn (maize). Also the name of the dish made from it.

potatoes, kipfler small, finger-shaped potato having a nutty flavour.

prawns also known as shrimp.

rice paper there are two products sold as rice paper. The one used in making confectionery is an edible, translucent glossy rice paper made from a dough made of water combined with the pith of an Asian shrub called the rice-paper plant (or rice-paper tree). Resembling a grainy sheet of paper, and whiter than the rice paper used as a spring roll wrapper, it is imported from Holland; never eat it uncooked.

rice paper wrappers (sheets) also known as banh trang. Made from rice paste and stamped into rounds. They are quite brittle and will break if dropped; when dipped momentarily in water they become pliable wrappers for fried food and uncooked vegetables.

sauce

chilli we use a hot Chinese variety made from bird's-eye chillies, salt and vinegar. Use sparingly to suit your taste.

fish also called nam pla or nuoc nam; made from pulverised salted fermented fish, most often anchovies. Has a pungent smell and strong taste; use sparingly.

hoisin a thick, sweet and spicy Chinese paste made from salted fermented soy beans, onions and garlic.

oyster a rich, brown sauce made from oysters and their brine, cooked with salt and soy sauce, and thickened with starches.

plum a thick, sweet and sour dipping sauce made from plums, vinegar, sugar, chillies and spices.

soy made from fermented soy beans. Several types are available in most supermarkets and Asian food stores.

sweet chilli a comparatively mild, Thai sauce made from red chillies, sugar, garlic and vinegar.

Tabasco an extremely fiery sauce made from vinegar, hot red chillies and salt.

tomato also known as ketchup or catsup; made from tomatoes, vinegar and spices.

shiitake mushrooms are large and meaty and often used as a substitute for meat. When dried, they are known as donko or dried chinese mushrooms; rehydrate before use.

sponge finger biscuits also known as savoiardi or savoy biscuits, lady's fingers or sponge fingers; Italian-style crisp fingers made from sponge cake mixture.

spring roll wrappers also called egg roll wrappers; they can be used for making gow gee and samosas as well as spring rolls.

tahini sesame seed paste available from Middle-Eastern food stores.

tandoori paste consisting of garlic, tamarind, ginger, coriander, chilli and spices.

turmeric a rhizome related to galangal and ginger; available fresh or powdered.

vietnamese mint not a mint at all, but a pungent, peppery narrow-leafed member of the buckwheat family.

wombok also known as peking cabbage, chinese cabbage or petsai; it is elongated in shape with pale green, crinkly leaves.

conversion chart

MEASURES

One Australian metric measuring cup holds approximately 250ml, one Australian metric tablespoon holds 20ml, one Australian metric teaspoon holds 5ml.

The difference between one country's measuring cups and another's is within a 2- or 3-teaspoon variance, and will not affect your cooking results. North America, New Zealand and the United Kingdom use a 15ml tablespoon. All cup and spoon measurements are level. The most accurate way of measuring dry ingredients is to weigh them. When measuring liquids, use a clear glass or plastic jug with metric markings.

We use large eggs with an average weight of 60g.

DRY MEASURES

METRIC	IMPERIAL
15g	½oz
30g	1oz
60g	2oz
90g	3oz
125g	4oz (¼lb)
155g	5oz
185g	6oz
220g	7oz
250g	8oz (½lb)
280g	9oz
315g	10oz
345g	11oz
375g	12oz (¾lb)
410g	13oz
440g	14oz
470g	15oz
500g	16oz (1lb)
750g	24oz (1½lb)
1kg	32oz (2lb)

LIQUID MEASURES

METRIC	IMPERIAL
30ml	1 fluid oz
60ml	2 fluid oz
100ml	3 fluid oz
125ml	4 fluid oz
150ml	5 fluid oz (¼ pint/1 gill)
190ml	6 fluid oz
250ml	8 fluid oz
300ml	10 fluid oz (½ pint)
500ml	16 fluid oz
600ml	20 fluid oz (1 pint)
1000ml (1 litre)	1¾ pints

LENGTH MEASURES

METRIC	IMPERIAL
3mm	⅛in
6mm	¼in
1cm	½in
2cm	¾in
2.5cm	1in
5cm	2in
6cm	2½in
8cm	3in
10cm	4in
13cm	5in
15cm	6in
18cm	7in
20cm	8in
23cm	9in
25cm	10in
28cm	11in
30cm	12in (1ft)

OVEN TEMPERATURES

These oven temperatures are only a guide for conventional ovens.
For fan-forced ovens, check the manufacturer's manual.

	°C (CELSIUS)	°F (FAHRENHEIT)	GAS MARK
Very slow	120	250	½
Slow	150	275 – 300	1 – 2
Moderately slow	160	325	3
Moderate	180	350 – 375	4 – 5
Moderately hot	200	400	6
Hot	220	425 – 450	7 – 8
Very hot	240	475	9

index

Are you missing some of the world's favourite cookbooks?

The Australian Women's Weekly cookbooks are available from bookshops, cookshops, supermarkets and other stores all over the world. You can also buy direct from the publisher, using the order form below.

MINI SERIES £3.50 190x138MM 64 PAGES

TITLE	QTY	TITLE	QTY	TITLE	QTY
4 Fast Ingredients		Drinks		Pasta	
15-minute Feasts		Easy Pies & Pastries		Potatoes	
50 Fast Chicken Fillets		Finger Food		Roast	
50 Fast Desserts		Fishcakes & Crispybakes		Salads	
50 Fast Prawns (Oct 07)		Gluten-free Cooking		Simple Slices	
After-work Stir-fries		Healthy Everyday Food 4 Kids		Simply Seafood	
Barbecue Chicken		Ice-creams & Sorbets		Skinny Food	
Bites		Indian Cooking		Spanish Favourites	
Bowl Food		Italian Favourites		Stir-fries	
Burgers, Rösti & Fritters		Jams & Jellies		Summer Salads	
Cafe Cakes		Japanese Favourites		Tagines & Couscous	
Cafe Food		Kebabs & Skewers		Tapas, Antipasto & Mezze	
Casseroles		Kids Party Food		Tarts	
Casseroles & Curries		Last-minute Meals		Tex-Mex	
Char-grills & Barbecues		Lebanese Cooking		Thai Favourites	
Cheesecakes, Pavlova & Trifles		Low-Fat Delicious		The Fast Egg	
Chinese Favourites		Malaysian Favourites		Vegetarian	
Christmas Cakes & Puddings		Mince		Vegie Main Meals	
Christmas Favourites (Oct 07)		Mince Favourites		Vietnamese Favourites	
Cocktails		Muffins		Wok	
Crumbles & Bakes		Noodles			
Cupcakes & Cookies		Noodles & Stir-fries			
Curries		Outdoor Eating			
Dips & Dippers		Party Food			
Dried Fruit & Nuts		Pickles and Chutneys		TOTAL COST £	

Photocopy and complete coupon below

Name _____

Address _____

_____ Postcode _____

Country _____ Phone (business hours) _____

Email*(optional) _____

*By including your email address, you consent to receipt of any email regarding this magazine, and other emails which inform you of ACP's other publications, products, services and events, and to promote third party goods and services you may be interested in.

I enclose my cheque/money order for £ _____ or please charge £ _____

to my: ☐ Access ☐ Mastercard ☐ Visa ☐ Diners Club

Card number | | | | | | | | | | | | | | |

3 digit security code *(found on reverse of card)* _____

Cardholder's signature _____ Expiry date ____ / ____

To order: Mail or fax - photocopy or complete the order form above, and send your credit card details or cheque payable to: Australian Consolidated Press (UK), 10 Scirocco Close, Moulton Park Office Village, Northampton NN3 6AP, phone (+44) (01) 604 642200, fax (+44) (01) 604 642300, e-mail books@acpuk.com or order online at www.acpuk.com

Non-UK residents: We accept the credit cards listed on the coupon, or cheques, drafts or International Money Orders payable in sterling and drawn on a UK bank. Credit card charges are at the exchange rate current at the time of payment.

All pricing current at time of going to press and subject to change/availability.
Postage and packing UK: Add £1.00 per order plus 75p per book.
Postage and packing overseas: Add £2.00 per order plus £1.50 per book. **Offer ends 31.12.2008**